JN061750

Surviving
in a Global World

Junji Nakagawa   Justin Charlebois

SEIBIDO

音声ファイルのダウンロード／ストリーミング

CD マーク表示がある箇所は、音声を弊社 HP より無料でダウンロード／ストリーミングすることができます。トップページのバナーをクリックし、書籍検索してください。書籍詳細ページに音声ダウンロードアイコンがございますのでそちらから自習用音声としてご活用ください。

https://www.seibido.co.jp

Surviving in a Global World

Preface

We live in a thrilling era because of drastic developments in technology and globalization. The traditional borders created by physical distance are diminishing. Consequently, we can easily contact people from across the globe and access information about different cultures. At the same time, there are various challenges we must face due to globalization and the fast pace of contemporary times. While technology can make it easy to contact others, people have different perspectives and values that would cause miscommunication. We wrote this textbook to help you lessen such miscommunication and navigate the complexities of a fast paced global world.

The textbook consists of 12 units. Each unit focuses on an aspect of life that you might encounter in a global world and is designed to give you real-world examples you may encounter. The units contain essays about the various challenges global citizens encounter. Each unit also provides exercises for you to practice the expressions that are used in the unit essays.

We emphasize developing the ability to think logically. The textbook will also help you develop your speaking, writing, and listening skills. The current global society demands that people can clearly express themselves in English. You might have the chance to work with native speakers of English and need to learn how to negotiate and make presentations in English. You might also have an opportunity to explain what the job involves in English to non-native speakers of English. To prepare for those occasions, we hope you would cultivate the skills described above through your English class.

A global society is not a distant reality, but it is the world you currently live in without realizing it. Developments in technology have made the world smaller and turned us all into global citizens. You are going to have many different opportunities to contribute to a global world. In order to thrive in this global society, you must make expressing your thoughts. It would also be important for you to spread the good aspects of Japan and Japanese views of things to the global world. It is our hope that this textbook will help you grow as a communicator and support your ability to contribute to the world as a global citizen.

Junji Nakagawa
Justin Charlebois

本書の構成と使い方について

Introduction

各 Unit で学ぶことを英文で紹介しています。授業が始まる前に目を通しておくと、Unit の目指しているゴールがより明確に把握できるでしょう。

Case Study

大学生活の場や社会に出たときに起こり得る異文化が交わる場面を想定した 4 コママンガです。マンガを読んだ後、4 コママンガの枠外の Question に対して、あなたがどのように考えるかを、個人あるいはグループとして英語で発表しましょう。

Key Vocabulary

次の Reading に出てくる語のうち、難易度が中程度の語彙を中心に取り上げています。選択肢は Reading で使われている文意に沿ったものを挙げていますので、エッセイを読むときの参考にしてみましょう。

Reading

350 〜 400 words で書かれたエッセイです。それぞれのパラグラフの内容を把握しながら読むことを心がけて、読解力を養っていきましょう。

Comprehension

Reading の理解度をみます。4 つの選択肢から正答を 1 つ選ぶ形式にしています。

Writing Practice

それぞれの Unit のエッセイの中から選んだ語句を使って、日本語を英語で表現します。完成した英文が、日本語を見てすぐに口頭で言えるようになることを目指しましょう。

Noteworthy Expressions

知っておくと便利な表現や役に立つ日常表現などを、Unit の内容に応じてコラム形式でまとめた「注目表現」です。下線部に語彙を補う作業などを通して、自己表現のためのヒントを学びましょう。

Listening Practice

問題解決がうまくいった会話の展開例や、説得力のある自己アピールができるような効果的な会話例を通して、Listening の力を伸ばしていきます。空欄の箇所は一つのまとまりとして聴き取るようにしましょう。

　発信できる自分になるトレーニングをすることを目指して、思考力を養い、英語で自分の考えを述べる場として、積極的に設問に挑戦していきましょう。与えられた課題については、問1では主に自分の意見を述べる、問2ではペア（またはクラス）で話し合う、という形式にしています。大きな声で、自信をもって発表しましょう。

　以上がそれぞれのセクションのおおまかな説明です。あなたはグローバル社会が必要としている貴重な人材の一人です。このテキストのさまざまなアクティビティを通して、グローバル市民の一員として素養を身につけ、発信することが得意なグローバル人材になる、グローバル社会に打って出られる人材になる、などの目標をもって、授業に取り組んでみましょう。

　最後になりましたが、本書の企画、出版にあたり、成美堂の宍戸貢氏に大変お世話になりました。心より感謝申し上げます。ありがとうございました。

My Progress Table

Number of Correct Answers				
Unit	Key Vocabulary	Comprehension	Review Quiz	Date
1	/10	/10	/10	/
2	/10	/10	/10	/
3	/10	/10	/10	/
4	/10	/10	/10	/
5	/10	/10	/10	/
6	/10	/10	/10	/
7	/10	/10	/10	/
8	/10	/10	/10	/
9	/10	/10	/10	/
10	/10	/10	/10	/
11	/10	/10	/10	/
12	/10	/10	/10	/

　自分の正答数を記入し、スコアを記録していきましょう。Unitのすべての項目をやり終えた日付をDate欄に記入しましょう。

Table of Contents

Globalization and the Global Society

グローバル社会って何？

We live in an era where people, products, and information move across the globe. Our world has become economically and culturally diverse due to ever-intensifying globalization. This age of globalization necessitates that people not only respect but also learn how to live with people who share different cultural values. We need to address the various challenges that accompany living and working together. Let's seize the opportunity to learn how to flourish in this global world.

Case Study

CD 02

First, look at the four-frame cartoon below, then discuss the question at the bottom of the cartoon with a partner or in small groups.

Emily and Hayato are college students in Japan. They are grabbing a coffee at a cafeteria.

Question Do you think that "hiring people from abroad would be a good strategy to solve the declining population issue in Japan"?

 **Key Vocabulary**

 03

Write the letter of the word or phrase with the closest meaning next to the appropriate vocabulary word.

1. thrive ( )   **5.** enable ( )   **9.** resident ( )
2. connection ( )   **6.** impact ( )   **10.** confidence ( )
3. expensive ( )   **7.** product ( )
4. likewise ( )   **8.** impression ( )

a. effect	**b.** allow	**c.** perception	**d.** pricey	**e.** relationship
f. goods	**g.** similarly	**h.** belief in oneself	**i.** flourish	**j.** inhabitant

 Reading

04~07

1 We live in an exciting time because of globalization. This word means that the physical borders created by countries are less restrictive. New developments in technology and convenient transportation methods have increased the opportunities for people to communicate from all over the world. Nowadays, people use computers to
5 make friends, do business, and learn about other cultures and ways of life. We must learn new ways of thinking and communicating so we can thrive in this era of globalization.

2 A global society is a one where people from across the globe are interconnected. These connections are formed through convenient international travel and developments in technology. In the past, it was very expensive and time-consuming to travel abroad,
10 but now we can easily visit or live in other countries. Likewise, the Internet has enabled people from different parts of the world to learn about each other and communicate.

3 Living in a global society has already impacted your life. Think of the popularity of foreign music and movies in Japan. Foreign movies and music videos are products of a global society. For example, some American movie stars are immigrants or from
15 immigrant families. Their clothes are not only produced in America, but also created by European designers. The movies themselves are often filmed outside the United States. Their audience is made up of people from all over the world, who will share their impressions of the movie through social media.

4 You should also be prepared to live in a global society. Learning to speak English well
20 is a necessary step to enter this global society. In your lifetime, you will use English to communicate with foreign tourists and residents in Japan. You will also use English to communicate with others through the Internet. Have confidence in your English ability since there is a good chance the person you speak with will also be a non-native speaker

of English. Don't worry about making small grammatical mistakes and proactively
25 express your opinion. You should also be confident about Japan and introduce Japanese
things such as manga, animation, and food to other people. It's a good idea to practice
your language skills, enhance your communication skills, and discuss topics about Japan
with others. As a result, you will be able to make contributions to a global society and
become a global citizen.

■ NOTES

physical border「地理的な境界線」 **restrictive**「制限的な」 **interconnected**「相互につながっている」
time-consuming「時間のかかる」 **social media**「ソーシャルメディア（インターネットを利用して双方向
のコミュニケーションを促進するサービスの総称）」 **there is a good chance**「という可能性が高い」
grammatical mistakes「文法上の誤り」 **proactively**「積極的に」 **enhance**「高める」
make contributions to「に貢献する」

Comprehension

Read the essay and complete the sentences with the correct choices.

1. In paragraph 1, the author says that physical borders are gradually _____.
   a. gaining national recognition
   b. having less significance
   c. disappearing
   d. becoming important

2. According to paragraph 2, a global society has made it possible to _____.
   a. connect with people from across the globe
   b. spend time and money to travel abroad
   c. visit other countries freely
   d. communicate with people from different parts of the world without the Internet

3. Based on paragraph 3, the correct statement is _____.
   a. foreign music and movies have little influence on Japanese people
   b. it's hard to buy clothes created by European designers in America
   c. American movies are made exclusively outside the United States
   d. social media enables people from all over the world to share their impressions
      of the movie

4. In order to prepare to live in a global society, all of the following are useful EXCEPT to
   _____.
   a. actively express your opinion
   b. use English to communicate with others through the Internet
   c. try to speak perfect English
   d. introduce Japanese things to other people

𝄢 **Writing Practice**

Rearrange the words and phrases in parentheses and make English sentences that correctly express the Japanese.

1. 多くの学生は、彼らが就活に関する国境を越えた情報交換のできるネットワークを望んでいる。
   Many students want a worldwide network that (information about / enables them / from across / to exchange / job-hunting) the globe.

   _____

   _____

2. ボブが日本の会社で働くことに興味を示す可能性は大いにある。
   There (at a Japanese company / in working / Bob will / is a good chance / be interested).

   _____

   _____

3. ソーシャルメディアを使って、私たちは共通の関心を持つ人を世界中から見つけることができる。
   With the use of social media, (who share / all over the globe / we can / a common interest / find people from).

   _____

   _____

4. わが社の社長は、地域の活性化に貢献し続けると言った。
   The president of our company said (the local community / we would / make contributions / continue to / to stimulate).

   _____

   _____

Noteworthy Expressions

グローバル vs インターナショナル

「グローバル」と「インターナショナル」。この2つの語の違いは何でしょうか。次のそれぞれのペアになっている日本文を比較しながら、英文の下線部に、下の選択肢から選んだ語句を補って、2つの語の意味の違いを英語で表現してみましょう。

1 「グローバル」は「グローブ（地球）」の形容詞形で、「地球規模の」という意味である。
"Global" is an adjective form of "globe" which means "_____."

「インターナショナル」は「インター（間で）」と「ナショナル（国の）」の合成語で「国家間の」という意味である。
"International" combines "inter-" (between or among) and "national (an adjective form of "nation"). It means "between or among _____."

2 「グローバル」は地球上にある問題について言及するときに使われる。
"Global" is used to refer to _____ that involve the whole world.

「インターナショナル」は国と国との結びつきに言及するときに使われる。
"International" is used to refer to the _____ between nations.

3 「グローバル」は「ボーダーレス」を意味しており、ヒト、モノ、カネ、文化、情報を自由にやり取りできる世界を表している。
"Global" means "borderless" and describes a world where we can freely exchange people, _____, money, culture, and information.

「インターナショナル」は「2つあるいはそれ以上の国に関する」という意味なので、相互関係は関係諸国だけに限定される。
"International" means "concerning two or more nations" so interaction is confined to the _____.

---

issues,   countries involved,   nations,   goods,   worldwide,
connections

▶◀ Listening Practice

 08

Listen to the conversation and fill in the blanks with the appropriate words based on the conversation.

Akina was an exchange student at Larry's college last semester. She returned to Japan, but they maintain their friendship through the Internet. They are chatting online.

Larry: Hey, Akina. We really miss you at our school.

Akina: Thanks. I miss the U.S., too. (   )?

Larry: Your presence here really made other students interested in Japan.

Akina: (   ).

Larry: Yeah, one of my (   ) Japanese. She's very interested in classical Japanese literature such as *The Tale of Genji*.

Akina: That's great. (   ) American literature as well. *The Great Gatsby* is now one of my favorite books. I think (   ).

Larry: That's true. Did you see the Hollywood movie?

Akina: I did, but (   ).

▲ Sharing Your Ideas

1. We live in a time when we are using various types of social media. What social media do you use? What do you use it for? Present answers to these questions to the class.
   1. What social media do you use most frequently?
   2. Why do you use it?
   3. Discuss the advantages and disadvantages of using it.

2. As globalization continues, growing numbers of people have become interested in Japan. Choose a Japan-related topic and explain it in English. You can discuss topics such as recommended sightseeing places, Japanese culture, Japanese food, traditional events in Japan or your area, Japanese pop culture, social games, manga, anime, cosplay, and Japanese traditions.

UNIT 2

How Do You Define a Global Citizen?

グローバル人材とはどんな人か

I n our diverse world, one might wonder what kinds of skills will be necessary to become a global citizen. One must be able to collaborate with people with diverse backgrounds and values. A global citizen must also be proactive and thus able to communicate with others about a range of topics. What skills do you think are necessary to become a global citizen? How do you think you can prepare to become a global citizen?

Case Study

 09

First, look at the four-frame cartoon below, then discuss the question at the bottom of the cartoon with a partner or in small groups.

Emily and Hayato are talking about their jobs in the future.

Question If you are Hayato, how do you respond to Emily's question in the 3rd panel?

_____

_____

 **Key Vocabulary**

Write the letter of the word or phrase with the closest meaning next to the appropriate vocabulary word.

1. perspective ( )	**5.** contribute ( )	**9.** opportunity ( )
2. desirable ( )	**6.** analyze ( )	**10.** cooperate ( )
3. essential ( )	**7.** assert ( )	
4. solution ( )	**8.** resource ( )	

> **a.** play a significant role   **b.** work together   **c.** insist   **d.** point of view   **e.** necessary
> **f.** tool   **g.** answer   **h.** examine   **i.** chance   **j.** suitable

Reading

1 In the dynamic era of globalization, people who live in this world are not only local citizens but also global citizens. Developments in technology have created opportunities for people in business and other fields to collaborate. Globalization is making the connections between different countries stronger than in the past and more people are
5 becoming global citizens. As a result, people are expected to have a more global perspective. This unit will encourage you to consider your role as a global citizen.

2 First, let's consider some of the desirable qualities for global citizens to have. Knowledge of other cultures is crucial. Globalization has made our world smaller and more connected, so people need an understanding of other cultures. Second, strong
10 written and spoken communication skills are essential. In order to increase your verbal communication skills, you should also learn how to form an opinion and express it. Your knowledge of other cultures and ability to express an original opinion will enable you to work successfully with others. People have different opinions and ideas, so you will need to learn how to exchange different opinions.

15 **3** With these things in mind, you should consider your role as a global citizen and how to prepare for that role. Global citizens need to be able to discuss various issues and find solutions to problems when dealing with people who have different views and opinions. You can actively contribute to globalization by working with people in your society to analyze the issues and state your opinions. Even if you feel that your opinion is not that
20 important, confidently assert your opinions without hesitation. These steps will help support your development as a global citizen.

4 The Internet and other media are great resources to help develop your ability to express your opinions and increase your knowledge of other cultures. To enhance your

communicative skills, you should have confidence in your English ability and discuss
25 interesting things you know about Japan. The most important thing is to use every
opportunity to communicate and learn about other people's perspectives and ways of
thinking. In our global world, we need global citizens who make every effort to
understand others, cooperate with a variety of people, and effortlessly adapt to new
environments.

■ NOTES

collaborate「共同して働く」**crucial**「とても重要な」**form an opinion**「意見を形にする」**original opinion**「独創的な意見」**without hesitation**「ためらわずに、遠慮せずに」**have confidence in**「に自信を持つ」**make every effort to**「～するためにあらゆる努力をする」**a variety of people**「いろいろな人たち」**adapt to**「に順応する」

🔁 Comprehension

Read the essay and complete the sentences with the correct choices.

1. Developments in technology have created opportunities for people to _____.
   a. work together
   b. compete against one another
   c. agree about everything
   d. combine business with other fields

2. Global citizens should have knowledge of _____.
   a. ways to provide different opinions and ideas
   b. values based on a society's culture
   c. both their own culture and other cultures
   d. how to express a conflicting opinion

3. To prepare for your role as a global citizen, you should learn to _____.
   a. defend your own opinion strongly
   b. respect other perspectives
   c. debate a particular topic
   d. speak several different languages

4. To become a more effective communicator, you should _____.
   a. not have too much pride in Japan
   b. talk about Japan with confidence
   c. do research about other cultures
   d. focus only on your spoken communication skills

Writing Practice

Rearrange the words and phrases in parentheses and make English sentences that correctly express the Japanese.

1. 私はためらわずに自分の意見を主張する自信があまりない。
   I don't really have (my opinions / hesitation / much confidence / without / in asserting).

   _____

   _____

2. 私たちのスクールカウンセラーは、新入生が大学生活に適応できる手助けをするために、あらゆる努力をしてくれる。
   Our school counselor (to help / every effort / makes / adjust to / new students) college life.

   _____

   _____

3. あなたが協力してくれると、私たちは時間通りに終えることができるのですが。
   I'm sure we'll be able to (with me / you'd / if / finish on time / cooperate).

   _____

   _____

4. 外国の文化圏での生活に順応するのは、時としてむずかしい。
   It is sometimes (foreign culture / hard / in a / to living / to adapt).

   _____

   _____

Noteworthy Expressions

グローバル人材に求められるもの

社会や企業が求めるグローバル人材像はさまざまです。一口にグローバル人材と言ってもイメージが湧かないと思います。求められるグローバル人材像とは何か。ここでは社会に求められるグローバル人材像の例をいくつか挙げてみました。日本文を参考にして、英語の下線部に、下の選択肢から適切な語句を選んで入れましょう。

1 さまざまな状況にうまく対応できる人
A person who can adjust to a wide _____ situations

2 強固な人間関係を築ける人
A person who can build solid _____ with people

3 専門領域を持っている人
A person who has an area of _____

4 異文化を理解できる人
A person who can _____ other cultures

5 前向きな姿勢の人
A person who has a positive _____

6 別の言語を学ぶ意欲がある人
A person who is _____ learn different languages

7 多様な背景をもつ人々とコミュニケーションのとれる人
A person who can communicate with people from _____

> diverse backgrounds,   expertise,   motivated to,   variety of,
> attitude,   appreciate,   relationships

Listen to the conversation and fill in the blanks with the appropriate words based on the conversation.

Hayato and Emily are talking about jobs in a global society in the future.

Hayato: This is an exciting time. Jobs that (　　　　　　　　　　)
will be created in the future.

Emily: (　　　　　　　　　　　　　　　　) do you think there
will be?

Hayato: Many companies will probably send their (　　　　　　　　　　).

Emily: That's true, but I also think that companies will use (　　　　　　
　　　　　　　) to speak with people from abroad.

Hayato: Employees who never leave their (　　　　　　　　　　) will still
need to learn about other cultures and languages.

Emily: They will also need to (　　　　　　　　　　) in this
global world.

Sharing Your Ideas

1. Choose the person you want to become from Noteworthy Expressions and express specific ways to become that person. (Example: I want to become a global person who can appreciate other cultures. To become that person, I'll try to study abroad during college.)

2. In the future, what kinds of jobs do you think will be available? Talk with your partner and then present your ideas to the class. (Example: An online instructor will be available.)

UNIT 3

You Can Become a Global Citizen

あなたもグローバルに活躍できる

As our world globalizes, people must learn how to broaden their own worldviews. In the future, you will have choices such as what you want to do and where you want to live. Regardless of where you work or live, you will make contributions to a global society. It will be exciting to widen your own perspective through being exposed to different values. This is a great opportunity for you to widen your vision for your own future. Why don't you learn more about how to become a global citizen?

 **Case Study**

 16

First, look at the four-frame cartoon below, then discuss the question at the bottom of the cartoon with a partner or in small groups.

Ms. Yoshimoto is a manager of a multinational company whose common language is English. She is trying to persuade her employee, Mr. Tanaka, to work overseas, but he doesn't want to leave Japan.

Question Imagine you are in Mr. Tanaka's place. How would you respond to Ms. Yoshimoto?

 **Key Vocabulary** 17

Write the letter of the word or phrase with the closest meaning next to the appropriate vocabulary word.

1. conduct ( ) **5.** occur ( ) **9.** regard ( )
2. employee ( ) **6.** outlook ( ) **10.** increase ( )
3. career ( ) **7.** broaden ( )
4. conference ( ) **8.** criticize ( )

a. job	**b.** viewpoint	**c.** evaluate	**d.** widen	**e.** consider
f. hold	**g.** take place	**h.** worker	**i.** expand	**j.** meeting

 Reading 18~22

1 The development of the Internet and other forms of technology has made our world smaller and more interconnected. We live in a time when everyone needs to become more internationally-minded. Even if you never leave Japan, you will need to communicate with various people through technology. For example, international
5 business meetings are conducted through video conferencing, and people use social media to communicate with people from other countries.

2 Companies will hire employees who can successfully communicate with people of different cultural backgrounds. Employees will also need to master the necessary communication skills required to spend part of their careers working abroad.
10 International conferences and meetings will occur through computer technology. A more global outlook is necessary to thrive in this century because the world has become globalized.

3 This new global world may seem unfamiliar to many people, but you can learn how to succeed in this world. The best way to broaden your own perspective is to practice the
15 various skills you will learn in this book. You can further widen your own worldview by keeping in mind a couple of other things.

4 Firstly, remember to keep an open-mind and not criticize other cultures. We will learn in this book that cultural customs and communication styles are very different in Japan and elsewhere. For example, while punctuality is very important in Japan, other cultures
20 regard punctuality more liberally, and lateness is not frowned upon. Likewise, formality is important in Japan, but other cultures are more relaxed. You may feel surprised when a meeting does not start exactly on time and people are informally dressed. If you are prepared to accept such unfamiliar situations, you will be able to manage them appropriately.

25 **5** Secondly, use various materials and media to increase your own knowledge of culture and communication. In the process, you will be able to apply your knowledge to communicate effectively with a variety of people. These suggestions will help you to become a more skilled communicator who can meet the demands of this increasingly global world. Now you are at the beginning of the journey toward becoming a global 30 citizen.

■ NOTES

become more internationally-minded「もっと世界に目を向けるようになる」**video conferencing**「ビデオ会議」**unfamiliar**「なじみがない」**worldview**「世界観」**punctuality**「時間厳守」**liberally**「寛大に」**be frowned upon**「ひんしゅくを買う」**formality**「形式にこだわること」**meet the demands**「要求に応じる」

Comprehension

Read the essay and complete the sentences with the correct choices.

1. With video conferencing, you don't need to _____.
   a. communicate with people from other countries
   b. become more internationally-minded
   c. use social media
   d. travel to attend meetings

2. Based on paragraph 2, the correct statement is that _____.
   a. companies should hire people of different cultural backgrounds to succeed in this century
   b. everyone has realized that the world has become globalized
   c. employees will be expected to master the communication skills that companies require
   d. international meetings and conferences will be held via computer technology

3. In paragraph 4, the author points out that Japanese culture values _____.
   a. punctuality   b. an informal dress code
   c. lateness   d. meetings

4. All of these tips would probably help someone become a global citizen EXCEPT to _____.
   a. keep an open-mind and not criticize other cultures
   b. learn that cultural customs and communication styles are similar everywhere
   c. use various materials and media to expand your knowledge about culture and communication
   d. utilize cultural knowledge to become a good communicator

Writing Practice

Rearrange the words and phrases in parentheses and make English sentences that correctly express the Japanese.

1. 私は観衆の前でスピーチをする必要があるときには緊張する。
   I become nervous (required to / a speech / in front of / I'm / make / when) an audience.

   _____

   _____

2. チップを渡すのはアメリカの文化では大切な習慣だ、ということを覚えておいてください。
   Keep (an important / that / is / in mind / custom / tipping) in American culture.

   _____

   _____

3. ヨーロッパを旅行中、私はいろいろな人と出会った。
   I (traveling / a variety of / while / met / in / people) Europe.

   _____

   _____

4. 我々がミーティングを設定する時はいつも、彼は必ず時間通りに来て私を待たせることがない。
   Whenever we arrange a meeting, he is always (never / waiting / me / and / keeps / on time).

   _____

   _____

Noteworthy Expressions

自己アピールをしよう

英語で自己アピールがしっかりできるように、自分の長所や得意分野を述べるときの言い方を、下の例文を参考にして学びましょう。日本語に合致するように、英語の下線部に、下の選択肢から適切な語句を選んで入れましょう。

1 責任感が強い
I have a strong sense of _____.

2 どんな困難に直面しても踏ん張れる
I can _____ whatever difficulties I face.

3 目的を達成するまで努力を続けられる
I can _____ to achieve my goal.

4 仲間と協力して働ける
I am good at _____ with my colleagues.

5 人と積極的にコミュニケーションがとれる
I am _____ in communicating with others.

6 コンピュータープログラミングに精通している
I am _____ in computer programming.

> proficient, cooperating, persevere, proactive, responsibility, hang in there

 **Listening Practice**

Listen to the conversation and fill in the blanks with the appropriate words based on the conversation.

Kathy is the manager of a company and is interviewing Akira for a position.

Kathy: What can you tell me about yourself?

Akira: I've always been a hard worker. I like to take on ( ).

Kathy: That's great. What are your greatest strengths and weaknesses?

Akira: My strength is that I ( )
and can easily adjust to a new environment. My weakness is
that I tend to ( ), which
can cause me stress.

Kathy: I think you'll find our employees are good at ( ).
Your ability to adjust to a new environment will ( )
because our workplace is busy, and employees are ( )
new skills.

 **Sharing Your Ideas**

1. Provide an example of something you can do in your daily life that would help you to prepare to live in a global society or learn about other cultures. Present your ideas to the class about what you are currently doing or what you'd like to do in the near future. (Example: I chat with overseas students on campus.)

2. In a global society, you will need to work with people from different backgrounds and professions. What do you think you should keep in mind to get along well with them? Use the following expressions to express your thoughts, then ask your partner his/her thoughts.
   While working with various people, I think I will need to _____. (Example: While working with various people, I think I will need to learn how to respect different views. How about you, Ken?)

Saying "Yes" or "No" Clearly

断るときは、はっきりと！

Do you say "yes" or "no" clearly when you speak English? Clearly expressing yourself is an essential skill that is necessary for you to thrive in a global society. Japanese people are not used to this style of communication, but you can learn it with some effort and practice. In this unit, let's consider the importance of making your intentions clear in business situations and daily life. Learning this skill will bring you one step closer to becoming a valuable global citizen.

Case Study

CD 24

First, look at the four-frame cartoon below, then discuss the question at the bottom of the cartoon with a partner or in small groups.

Mr. Smith, an American salesperson, is visiting Mr. Yamada, a Japanese distributor, and is asking him to carry a new product. Mr. Yamada does not find Mr. Smith's offer that appealing.

Question Based on "I'll think about it," what will Mr. Smith probably think?

_____

_____

 **Key Vocabulary**

Write the letter of the word or phrase with the closest meaning next to the appropriate vocabulary word.

1. influence ( )   **5.** interpret ( )   **9.** hesitate ( )
2. adjust ( )   **6.** conflict ( )   **10.** beverage ( )
3. honesty ( )   **7.** criticism ( )
4. individual ( )   **8.** insult ( )

a. dispute	**b.** say something mean	**c.** adapt	**d.** critique	**e.** affect
f. understand	**g.** person	**h.** be reluctant	**i.** drink	**j.** frankness

Reading

1 In our global world, communication between people with different backgrounds is common. Naturally, our cultural backgrounds influence how we interact with each other. A difficult aspect of global communication is learning how certain cultures view indirect and direct communication styles and how to adjust your style to fit the situation.

5 **2** "Don't mince words" and "say what you mean" are American English expressions that reflect the importance of directness in American culture. Since people view themselves as individuals rather than as members of a group, they use a direct style of communication. They value frankness because they do not share the same cultural values and cannot easily interpret indirect expressions. People regard expressing a different 10 opinion from others as a way to solve problems. Conflict is seen as a matter of course and a normal part of conversation. However, since speaking too bluntly or assertively could hurt others, people remember to be polite when saying "no" or expressing a different opinion.

3 In cultures like Japan, an indirect communication style is frequently used. The 15 expression of direct criticism is avoided because it could insult the other person and damage the relationship. People view themselves as members of a group and they share many of the same cultural values. Since group harmony is valued, speakers are careful to avoid expressing disagreement or negative evaluations. Even if people disagree with an opinion, they usually hesitate to directly disagree because conflict damages relationships. 20 For example, a Japanese person might say, "I'll think about it" as an alternative to a direct refusal. This expression is too vague in English, and many people would assume that the person might really need some time to think it through.

4 These cultural differences can cause miscommunication to occur. For example, at a

Japanese-style restaurant, a group of people usually order the same beverage and several
25   dishes of food to share even if someone dislikes one of the items served. In the U.S. and
other Western cultures, a person politely expresses his/her preference, and the other
people would not be offended that he/she declined one of the dishes. The person's
forthrightness would be appreciated by the others and their feelings would not be hurt.
We should remember that the same principle applies to a business meeting at a global
30   company.

■ *NOTES*

interact「交流する、ふれあう」**global communication**「グローバルな環境で行われるコミュニケーション」
don't mince words「歯に衣着せぬ物言いをする」**frankness**「率直であること」**as a matter of course**「当
然のこととして」**speaking too bluntly or assertively**「あまりずけずけものを言ったりはっきりと言い過
ぎたりすること」**evaluation**「評価」**think through**「熟考する、じっくりと考える」**forthrightness**「率
直さ」

Comprehension

Read the essay and complete the sentences with the correct choices.

1. One difficult aspect of global communication is _____.
     a. the environment
     b. learning how to modify your communication style
     c. disagreeing with other people
     d. remembering how to use new technology

2. In America, it is a good idea to express disagreement _____.
     a. bluntly
     b. politely
     c. indirectly
     d. anytime

3. Japanese people usually avoid expressing direct negative evaluations because _____.
     a. they share a similar background and opinions
     b. they lack confidence in their English ability
     c. criticism is important
     d. harmony is valued

4. At a social event in America, people usually _____.
     a. decline one of the dishes before they accept it
     b. express no preference
     c. order what they like
     d. let the host order food for everyone

Writing Practice

Rearrange the words and phrases in parentheses and make English sentences that correctly express the Japanese.

1. きみは過去より未来に目を向けるべきだ。
   You should (the future / than / look to / rather / the past).

   _____

   _____

2. たとえ完全には理解できなくても、彼の生き方を尊重しませんか。
   Why don't you (his lifestyle / completely understand / even if / respect / you can't) it?

   _____

   _____

3. ご提案をよく考えて、2週間以内にご連絡します。
   I'll (your proposal / within / you / and contact / think through) two weeks.

   _____

   _____

4. あなたに言ったことは、例外なく世界中の誰にでも当てはまります。
   What I told (applies to / you / without / everyone / in the world) exception.

   _____

   _____

Noteworthy Expressions

断るときは、はっきりと！

日本では、丁寧に断るための表現として「考えておきます」(I'll think about it.) と言うことがありますが、グローバル社会では、「考えておく」は「時間をかけて考えてから返事をする」という意味で解釈されることが多くあります。そこで誤解を招かないように、"I'll think about it." をもっと明確な言い方にしてみましょう。日本文を参考にして、英語の下線部に、下の選択肢から適切な語句を選んで入れましょう。

1 もうちょっと考える時間が必要です。後で連絡します。
   I need _____ time to think about this. Let me get back to you.

2 真剣に考えてみます。水曜日までにご連絡します。
   I'll seriously consider it. I'll be in _____ with you by Wednesday.

3 ご提案を内部で検討してみます。数日中に折り返し連絡します。
   I'd like to have _____ with my colleagues about your offer. I'll get back to you in a few days.

4 せっかくですが、ご提案を辞退申し上げます。
   I'm sorry to say this, but I must _____ your offer.

5 申し訳ございませんが、お受けできません。
   I'm sorry, but I've decided not to _____ your proposal.

6 残念ですが、今回はご要望にお応えできません。
   Unfortunately, we are unable to _____ to your request at this time.

---

a discussion,　accept,　touch,　decline,　some more,　respond

Listen to the conversation and fill in the blanks with the appropriate words based on the conversation.

Elizabeth and her friends plan to see a movie this weekend. She invites Haruto to join them.

Elizabeth: Hey, Haruto.

Haruto: Hi, Elizabeth.

Elizabeth: (   ) plan to see a movie
this weekend. Do you want to (   )?

Haruto: That sounds like (   ), but I want
to catch up on my studying this weekend. I'd (   )
next time.

Elizabeth: No problem. (   ) another time.

Haruto: Sure. (   ).

Sharing Your Ideas

1. What do you keep in mind when you refuse? Give an example that you think is important to the class. (Example: I usually use polite words and refuse directly but diplomatically.)

2. Your friend invites you to attend an event by saying something like, "Why don't we (go see the college football game) this weekend?" or he/she makes a similar invitation. Change the expressions in parentheses and practice how to decline an invitation with your partner. (Example: -Why don't we go see the art festival this weekend? -Actually, I think I'll stay home this weekend. Thanks for asking me anyway.)

Start Conversations with a Nice Compliment

人をほめることは、とても大事

While it is rare to directly praise someone in Japan, praise is used in other countries to create a sense of closeness. If you are not used to giving and receiving compliments, you may feel embarrassed being praised so much. In this unit, you will learn about the importance of praising others and how to do this. Compliments are used in conversation to create close relationships with others.

Case Study

 31

First, look at the four-frame cartoon below, then discuss the question at the bottom of the cartoon with a partner or in small groups.

Sakura is a newly hired employee at a global company. Her boss, John, is complimenting her because she is doing excellent work.

Question How do you think John would interpret Sakura's responses in the 3rd and 4th panel?

_____

_____

 **Key Vocabulary** 32

Write the letter of the word or phrase with the closest meaning next to the appropriate vocabulary word.

1. compliment ( )   **5.** outfit ( )   **9.** effective ( )

2. appearance ( )   **6.** latest ( )   **10.** reply ( )

3. personality ( )   **7.** jealous ( )

4. possession ( )   **8.** flow ( )

---

a. character   **b.** clothing   **c.** something that you have or own   **d.** newest

e. envious   **f.** nice comment   **g.** successful   **h.** proceed   **i.** answer   **j.** looks

 Reading 33~36

1 In Western countries, complimenting other people is a common way to promote smooth communication and is important to communicate effectively in a global world. Learning this useful communication skill can be difficult for many Japanese because of cultural differences.

5   **2** In English, compliments are used in conversations to create a close feeling between speakers. People compliment others' appearance, ability, or personality. For example, "I really love your sweater" or "You speak English very well." One appropriate way to respond to the compliment is to accept it with sincere gratitude. These compliments about appearance or ability may make Japanese feel embarrassed, but they should get
10   comfortable both receiving and giving compliments. Although learning this style may be difficult, it is crucial for Japanese to acquire the ability to respond properly.

3 Let's learn some common ways to make compliments and compliment responses. The purpose of complimenting is to communicate, so you don't have to take things too seriously. One easy way to compliment is to praise someone's appearance or possessions.
15   For example, you could say "Your outfit looks really nice. Is it new?" or "Is that the latest cell phone? I'm jealous." In both examples, the person will start talking about the possession and you can ask more questions about it, so the conversation will continue to flow. You can also express your opinion about certain brands of clothes or other items, so the conversation will continue. Do not worry about speaking perfect English. The person
20   is just happy to carry on a conversation with you.

4 Compliments also facilitate communication at international business meetings. Business people often use small talk during meetings to get to know each other. You may not know how to start a conversation with new people, so you could give someone a

---

compliment to get the conversation started. You should also learn how to reply to a
25 compliment correctly if someone praises you. Remember to avoid Japanese-style
responses and try to learn the Western style. This is an effective method to make the
conversation and meeting progress naturally. Expressing modesty and politeness in
conversation is essential in Japanese society. However, in order to succeed in a global
world, people must learn how to compliment and reply appropriately.

■ NOTES

promote smooth communication「会話を円滑なものにする」 **feel embarrassed**「気まずい思いをする」
carry on a conversation with「と会話を続ける」 **small talk**「(軽い) おしゃべり、世間話」 **facilitate**「容
易にする」 **modesty and politeness**「慎み深さや礼儀正しさ」

Comprehension

Read the essay and complete the sentences with the correct choices.

1. In Western countries, complimenting is important because it _____.
   a. promotes smooth communication
   b. prevents a business relationship
   c. produces a difficult situation
   d. provides ways to learn cultural differences

2. The author says that Japanese may feel _____ when praised.
   a. puzzled
   b. more relaxed
   c. confident
   d. a sense of gratitude

3. Compliments about person's possessions are _____ in Western-style communication.
   a. uncommon
   b. rare
   c. something trivial
   d. suitable

4. It can be inferred from the passage that one of the Japanese-style responses to
   compliments could be _____
   a. "Thank you. That's very kind of you."
   b. "Thank you, but that's not true."
   c. "I appreciate your compliment."
   d. "I'm glad to hear that."

Writing Practice

Rearrange the words and phrases in parentheses and make English sentences that correctly express the Japanese.

1. 私のブログに関する彼のコメントに、私は気まずい思いをした。
   His comment (feel / made / embarrassed / on my blog / me).

   _____

   _____

2. 私たちはその問題について話し合いを続けて、よい結論に達した。
   We carried on (a good conclusion / a conversation / came to / about the issue / and).

   _____

   _____

3. きみのことをもっと知るチャンスが欲しい。
   I'd really (to get / you better / to know / have the opportunity / like to).

   _____

   _____

4. 先日オープンしたばかりの美容院で、髪を短く切ってもらうつもりです。
   I'm going to (cut short / at the / get / that just / hair salon / my hair) opened the other day.

   _____

   _____

Noteworthy Expressions

ほめ上手になる！

英語圏では日常会話で当たり前のようにほめます。挨拶代わりに相手の外観をほめたり、人柄、ファッションセンス、アイディア、何かを成し遂げたりしたときなど、素敵だなと思ったことを素直に伝えます。ほめ言葉は単に相手を称賛するためだけでなく、そこから会話を弾ませていく糸口にもなります。そこで、ふだんからほめ言葉のフレーズをインプットしておくと、臨機応変にその場にふさわしいほめ言葉が出てきて、会話が楽しくなります。下の例文をみて、英語の下線部に、下の選択肢から適切な語句を選んで入れましょう。

1 すごいなぁ！ よくやった！
   Great! You did a terrific _____!

2 その服、オシャレだね。
   Your outfits are _____.

3 センスいいなぁ。
   You've got amazing _____!

4 きみはとても優秀なスタッフだ。
   You're really _____ staff member.

5 あなたってかっこよくて、やさしくて、とても頭がいいわね。
   You're cool, gentle and very _____.

6 きみのスピーチにはとても感銘を受けたよ。
   I was very _____ with your speech.

| impressed, | an excellent, | job, | smart, | taste, | stylish |

Listening Practice

 37

Listen to the conversation and fill in the blanks with the appropriate words based on the conversation.

Masaki is the manager at an international company and Sarah is the assistant manager. Sarah arrives in Masaki's office for a meeting.

Masaki: Hi, Sarah. I really love (   ).

Sarah: Thank you. I'm glad you like it. (   ) to surprise my fiancé.

Masaki: I'm sure (   ).

Sarah: I like your tie.

Masaki: Thanks. (   ) from my daughter.

Sarah: Wonderful! (   )?

Masaki: Before I answer your question, shall we talk about the proposal (   )?

Sharing Your Ideas

1. A friend from overseas asks you why Japanese people are modest even when they are praised. Express your views about this topic. (Example: Because they don't want to give the impression that they have much self-confidence.)

2. With your partner, find at least three positive things about the other person and practice praising each other. (Example: -You're very kind to others. -Thank you. I always admire your ability to express your feelings frankly.)

30   UNIT 5

UNIT 6 Why Can't People Read the Atmosphere?

察してもらうのはムリ

Communication gaps will most likely occur between people with different cultural backgrounds. The chances of miscommunication occurring are greater when one culture values implicit communication and the other one values explicit communication. The person from the culture where implicit communication is commonplace will face situations where he/she must explain everything in words. This unit will help you consider how to overcome the various challenges involved with living in a global society.

Case Study

First, look at the four-frame cartoon below, then discuss the question at the bottom of the cartoon with a partner or in small groups.

Shohei and Jim are roommates. Shohei is cleaning up their messy room now, but Jim is relaxing on the sofa.

Question What do you think of Jim's reaction in the 4th panel?

_____

_____

 **Key Vocabulary**

 39

Write the letter of the word or phrase with the closest meaning next to the appropriate vocabulary word.

1. immigrant   (   )   5. maintain   (   )   9. resolve   (   )
2. diverse   (   )   6. expectation (   )   10. deliver   (   )
3. atmosphere (   )   7. gesture   (   )
4. similar   (   )   8. preference (   )

| **a.** find the answer to | **b.** alike | **c.** body language | **d.** different | **e.** convey |
| **f.** assumption | **g.** liking | **h.** settler | **i.** mood | **j.** keep |

 Reading

40~43

1 Immigrants with different cultural backgrounds settled in the United States. Many of the immigrants were originally from Europe, so they shared some cultural and religious traditions, but since Europe is still very diverse, people did not share the exact same background. One result of this diversity was that people learned to communicate directly
5 and were not expected to figure out the meaning of words based on their own interpretations.

2 "Reading between the lines" or "reading the atmosphere" is an important social skill in Japan. Japan is a country where people share a similar cultural background and use the same communication style. People avoid disagreement so they can maintain harmony. A
10 related social norm is that people should not have to specify the exact meaning of the message they are trying to communicate. There is an expectation that the other person or people can interpret the speaker's meaning.

3 The indirect style has both merits and demerits. A good point is that people learn to become sensitive to the message others are communicating. There is no need to "spell
15 everything out" because people interpret the meaning behind the words. A drawback of this style is that there is a chance that people will miscommunicate. The chance for miscommunication to occur is even higher now that a large amount of communication occurs through technology. When we communicate with computers, we cannot interpret facial expressions, gestures, and other body language.

20 **4** There are two points Japanese can keep in mind to communicate successfully in a global world. First, you should express your opinion and preferences in a polite, direct manner. Do not worry if someone disagrees with your idea or opinion. In a diverse culture, it is natural for people to have different opinions. Second, talk to someone

directly if you want to resolve a problem or issue. While it is common to use an
25 intermediary to deliver a message to someone in Japan, this style is viewed unfavorably
in English-speaking countries. The best way to resolve any issue is to speak with the
person directly and openly. Japanese people who work in a global society need to not
only read the atmosphere but also get used to a more direct method of communication.

■ NOTES

settle in「住みつく」**diversity**「多様性」**figure out**「理解する」**social skill**「社会的技能（他人と良い関係を築き、社会に適応するために必要な能力）」**related**「関連した」**social norm**「社会規範（社会で当たり前と考えられている行動様式のこと）」**should not have to spell out**「はっきり述べる必要はない」**become sensitive to**「に敏感になる」**drawback**「欠点」**there is a chance that**「という可能性がある」**now that**「今や～だから」**keep in mind**「心に留めておく」**intermediary**「仲介者」**unfavorably**「好ましくなく」

🗩 Comprehension

Read the essay and complete the sentences with the correct choices.

1. Immigrants from Europe to the U.S. learned _____.
   a. direct ways of communication
   b. words based on their own interpretations
   c. to share the same background
   d. to understand the meaning of words in the same way

2. Since Japanese people share a similar cultural background, they _____.
   a. need to clearly say everything in words
   b. can exactly interpret the speaker's meaning every time
   c. consider "reading between the lines" to be an important social skill
   d. expect a direct communication style from others

3. One of the demerits of the indirect style is that _____.
   a. people interpret the meaning behind the words
   b. people become sensitive to the message others are communicating
   c. the possibility to miscommunicate is higher
   d. a lot of communication occurs through technology

4. To successfully communicate in a global world, all of the following are mentioned in paragraph 4 EXCEPT you _____.
   a. should express your opinion and preferences in a polite, direct manner
   b. don't have to worry if someone disagrees with your idea or opinion
   c. have to use an intermediary to deliver a message to someone
   d. need to get used to a more direct method of communication

Rearrange the words and phrases in parentheses and make English sentences that correctly express the Japanese.

1. 私には、空気を読むという意味がよく分からない。
   I can't (means / reading / what / figure out / the atmosphere).

   _____

   _____

2. 彼は支持者を説得するために、詳しくその計画を説明しなければならなかった。
   He had to (in detail / the plan / the supporters / spell out / to persuade).

   _____

   _____

3. 英語の会話力が上達したので、私は仕事にもっと自信がもてるようになった。
   I feel more confident (my speaking skills / now that / have improved / at work / in English).

   _____

   _____

4. その会社と交渉するときに、心に留めておくことは何かありますか。
   Is there anything (negotiating with / in mind / when / to keep / the company)?

   _____

   _____

Noteworthy Expressions

意見は率直に分かりやすく

Reading の中に出てくる "You should express your opinion and preferences in a polite, direct manner." と "Talk to someone directly if you want to resolve a problem or issue." について、自分の意見や問題を解決するときの、丁寧で率直に伝える表現をいくつか挙げてみました。日本文を参考にして、英語の下線部に下の選択肢から適切な語句を選んで入れましょう。

1 あなたの言っていることは分かりますが、一番いいプランだとは、やはり思えません。（ミーティングで）

I understand what you're saying, but I _____ that is not the best plan.

2 おっしゃることがよく分かりませんが、どういう意味でしょうか。（ディスカッション中に）

I don't quite _____ you. What exactly do you mean?

3 申し訳ありません、あなたの言っていることには同意できません。（ディスカッション中に）

I'm afraid I have to _____ with you.

4 音楽の音量を下げてもらえませんか？（隣人に）

Would you mind _____ down your music?

5 きみが宵っ張りなのは知っているけど、夜はもう少し静かにしてもらえないだろうか。（ルームメートに）

I know you are a night owl, but could you be a little _____ at night?

6 誘ってくれてありがとう、でも予定がいっぱいなんだ。（友人に）

Thanks for the invitation, but my schedule is completely _____.

turning,	booked up,	quieter,	follow,	still feel,	disagree

 **Listening Practice**

Listen to the conversation and fill in the blanks with the appropriate words based on the conversation.

Keiko is doing a homestay in the U.S. and is talking with her host father, Bill, at dinner.

Keiko: The dinner was really delicious. Thanks for (

).

Bill: (   ) yet. Sally made

us some cheesecake for dessert.

Keiko: (   ) and think I'll pass on

dessert tonight.

Bill: No problem. (   )

watching a movie with us tonight?

Keiko: Actually, I'm pretty tired and (   ). It was a busy

week.

Bill: (   ).

Keiko: Sorry, but I'm really too tired to watch a movie.

▲▲ **Sharing Your Ideas**

1. How do you respond to an opinion that's different from yours? Make a sample sentence and present it to the class. (Example: I understand your opinion, but I feel differently.)

2. We have learned that when we need someone's help in a global society, it is appropriate to ask the person directly rather than expect him/her to sense our needs. Take turns discussing the next two questions with your partner. First, what do you say when you need help? Second, how do you offer a person help? (Example: 1. -I need your help. -Sure. how can I help you? 2. -Can I help you? -Oh, thanks. Could you show me the way to the bus stop?)

UNIT 7 Don't Be Afraid to Make Mistakes

失敗を糧に立ち上がれ

Making mistakes is an inevitable part of our daily lives. The chances of making mistakes increase especially when you are overseas because of language or cultural differences. There is no need to be concerned about making mistakes. In this age of globalization, the ability to overcome these difficulties is a great skill to learn. With an "I can do it" attitude, you can rise to these various challenges and become a global citizen in the process.

▼ Case Study

CD 45

First, look at the four-frame cartoon below, then discuss the question at the bottom of the cartoon with a partner or in small groups.

Yuji is talking to his classmate, Olivia, during class. The students just received the results of their mid-term examination.

Question What suggestions would you propose for Yuji to express the meaning of "FIGHT" and "REVENGE"?

 **Key Vocabulary**

Write the letter of the word or phrase with the closest meaning next to the appropriate vocabulary word.

1. stimulating ( )   5. break (noun) ( )   9. notice ( )
2. encourage ( )   6. attentive ( )   10. gradually ( )
3. converse ( )   7. achieve ( )
4. consequently ( )   8. observe ( )

a. as a result	**b.** little by little	**c.** concentrated	**d.** watch	**e.** attain
f. support	**g.** discover	**h.** interesting	**i.** talk	**j.** rest

 Reading   47~50

1 Learning how to be a global citizen is a stimulating but difficult process. We need to learn how to express ourselves in another language and how to interact with different people. It is natural to make mistakes in the process. This unit will encourage you to learn how to develop as a global citizen by making mistakes.

5 **2** There are several cultural stumbling blocks that make successful communication hard. For example, it is very difficult for many Japanese to learn how to converse in English. Some Western people speak very quickly and talk only about themselves. Consequently, Japanese feel like they "cannot get a word in edgewise" because there is never a break in the conversation. They keep hoping the other people will ask them a question, but that
10 does not always occur. At the same time, Western people might feel that the other person is not fully engaged in the conversation and form the negative impression that Japanese are not attentive. This cultural misunderstanding results from not understanding the conversational style of another culture.

3 Robert Kennedy once said that "only those who dare to fail greatly can ever achieve
15 greatly." The way you can learn how to communicate successfully with new people in English is not to worry about making mistakes. In order to achieve success, we must be willing to make mistakes. To promote your success, you should observe how people interact with each other. You will notice that they freely talk and are not so concerned about content of what they are saying. The most important thing is to show that you care
20 about and are interested in the other person.

4 You can gradually learn how to use this style by asking questions. At first it is natural to feel uncomfortable talking about yourself and expressing your opinions. Therefore, you should ask questions to show your interest and gradually you will be able to express

yourself and join the conversation. Try to follow these simple guidelines and you will
25 become a successful communicator even in another language.

■ *NOTES*
stumbling blocks「障害」**get a word in edgewise**「口をはさむ、うまく会話に割り込む」**is engaged in the conversation**「会話に熱中している」**result from**「に起因する」**Robert Kennedy**「(1925-1968) ロバート・ケネディー（第 35 代米国合衆国大統領ジョン・F・ケネディの実弟）」**dare to**「恐れずに～する」**care about**「気にかける、思いやる」**interact**「交流する」**guideline**「ガイドライン、指針」

Comprehension

Read the essay and complete the sentences with the correct choices.

1. When you are aiming to be a global citizen, you _____.
   a. will promptly learn how to express yourself in another language
   b. could naturally encounter an opportunity to make mistakes
   c. should interact with people all around the world
   d. might avoid making mistakes

2. When Japanese are not engaged in the conversation, Western people feel that they are _____.
   a. waiting for a question from somebody
   b. afraid of interrupting the conversation
   c. eager to join the discussion
   d. not paying close attention to the conversation

3. To communicate well with new people, what truly matters to you is to _____.
   a. show that you are interested in the other person
   b. worry about making mistakes
   c. focus on the content of their conversation
   d. promote your success

4. "This style" in the fourth paragraph includes all of the following EXCEPT _____.
   a. talking about yourself
   b. expressing your opinions
   c. asking questions to show your interest
   d. failing at communicating in another language

Rearrange the words and phrases in parentheses and make English sentences that correctly express the Japanese.

1. 私たちは最新のOS（オペレーティングシステム）に乗り換えているところだ。
   We're (to a / switching over / operating system / brand-new / in the process of).

   _____

   _____

2. 私は友だちと話に熱中していたので、電車を乗り過ごしてしまった。
   Since (a conversation / engaged in / my friend / I was / with), I missed my station.

   _____

   _____

3. 地球温暖化は、温室効果から生じると考えられている。
   Global (is thought / from / to result / the greenhouse effect / warming).

   _____

   _____

4. 私のことを気にかけてくれるあなたのような友だちがいてくれて、とてもうれしいです。
   I'm (like you / a friend / very glad / who cares / to have) about me.

   _____

   _____

Noteworthy Expressions

和製英語は自然な英語表現で

和製英語（Japanese-made English）とは、海外の文化や言葉を日本流に変えて作られた英語風の日本語のことです。日本以外では意味が伝わりません。英語でコミュニケーションをとるときに、そのまま会話や文章の中で使うと、（Case Study でみたように）思わぬ失敗や誤解を生み出すこともあります。そこで、ふだん使っている英語っぽい表現も、もしかしたらそれは和製英語かも、と見直すようにして、自然な英語表現を身につけていきましょう。
次の日本文の下線部分は、そのまま英語にしても通じない和製英語です。それと同じ意味を表す英語の語句を下の選択肢から選んで、英語の下線部に入れましょう。

1. 私はマイペースで英語を勉強している。
   I'm studying English at my _____.

2. 私は英語力をレベルアップしたい。
   I want to _____ my English ability.

3. 力士は勝ってもガッツポーズをしたり飛び上がって喜んだりしない。
   A sumo wrestler doesn't _____ or jump for joy after a victory.

4. 近くにコインランドリーはありませんか？
   Is there a _____ near here?

5. レンジで 30 秒間チンするだけで、はい出来上がり！
   Just put it in the _____ for 30 seconds, and it's ready to eat!

6. ペットボトルによる廃棄物を減らすために水筒を使用しよう。
   Try to use a thermos to reduce the waste caused by _____ bottles.

---

plastic, improve, own pace, laundromat, microwave, pump his fists

Listen to the conversation and fill in the blanks with the appropriate words based on the conversation.

Takeru and Chloe, his co-worker, are having a chat in the office break room.

Takeru: ( ).

Chloe: What happened?

Takeru: ( ) this Friday with Ms. Davis. I forgot that I made an appointment to meet with Mr. Brown ( ) on Friday.

Chloe: Oh, no!

Takeru: How do you suggest that ( )?

Chloe: Well, if I were you, ( ) to Mr. Brown. I suggest that you call Ms. Davis to apologize and then ( ).

▲ **Sharing Your Ideas**

1. We have learned we shouldn't be afraid of making mistakes when speaking English. As a next step to make the conversation come alive, what do you want to keep in mind and put into practice? Express your thoughts to the class with the help of what you have learned from the essay. (Example: I learned that I don't have to lose my confidence even if my English skills are poor.)

2. Someone says something to you and you can't understand what he/she means. If you pretend to understand what he/she is talking about, it might lead to a communication breakdown. You should confirm that there is no miscommunication. How do you ask the person to repeat what he/she said? Practice the conversation with your partner. (Example: -Sorry. I couldn't catch what you said. Could you say it again? -Sure. You need to report to Sato-san if you're late for work.)

UNIT 8 Develop the Ability to Express Your Thoughts

自己主張をする

Developing the ability to express yourself is a crucial part of becoming a global citizen. In your lifetime, you will encounter various people through technology or face-to-face meetings. Since people have different perspectives and backgrounds, the best way to avoid miscommunication is by learning how to directly express yourself. This unit will teach you some concrete ways to improve your ability to express yourself.

▼ Case Study

🎧 CD 52

First, look at the four-frame cartoon below, then discuss the question at the bottom of the cartoon with a partner or in small groups.

Ken is studying at a university in the U.S. and is talking with a classmate, Susan, after class.

Question How would you respond to Susan's last question?

_____

_____

 **Key Vocabulary** 53

Write the letter of the word or phrase with the closest meaning next to the appropriate vocabulary word.

1. struggle ( )   **5.** military ( )   **9.** strategy ( )

2. appropriate ( )   **6.** controversial ( )   **10.** reduce ( )

3. awkward ( )   **7.** complex ( )

4. current ( )   **8.** unique ( )

a. complicated   **b.** present-day   **c.** cut down   **d.** make a great effort   **e.** special
f. embarrassing   **g.** self-defense force   **h.** proper   **i.** disputed   **j.** method

 Reading   54~57

1 Many Japanese people struggle to find appropriate conversational topics. They feel awkward and uncomfortable when they first meet people and need to make small talk. Western people often talk about current events. They might say to you, "Have you heard about this recent event?" If you don't know about it, then simply say, "No, I haven't.
5 Could you tell me about it?" While they are speaking, you should not only ask questions but also express your opinions and feelings. You don't have to feel bad at all even if someone disagrees with your opinion. The speaker might add, "Don't take it personally," an expression commonly used in English. It means the speaker is not expressing dislike toward you but conveying his/her views in general.

10 **2** Let's consider a conversation about international issues. For example, what would you say in response to this question, "Do you think that Japan should have a strong military?" This is a controversial topic. If you really have not thought about it, then say, "That's an extremely complex issue. I don't feel that I know enough about it to offer my view." You can then offer an opinion or a perspective on a related topic, "I do think that since we
15 live in a time of globalization, Japan should also play a crucial role in world affairs. I hope that more up-and-coming entrepreneurs will find unique ways to introduce Japanese products such as Japanese-style convenience stores to the international market."

3 On the other hand, there are times when a person does not want to offer an opinion. In these cases, you can say, "That's a matter I'd rather not talk about" or "That's a personal
20 question." However, in most situations, you should try and respond to questions, offer opinions, and engage with people in conversation.

4 One purpose of communication is to express who you are to the other person. Western people use language to get acquainted with each other. Therefore, it is a good idea to

learn some of the strategies discussed above so that you can express yourself to them. In
25 our global world, we can gradually reduce cultural misunderstandings by both expressing
ourselves and respecting the opinions of others.

■ **NOTES** ───────────────────────────────────

conversational topic「話のネタ、会話の話題」**feel awkward and uncomfortable**「気まずさと居心地の悪さを覚える」**in response to**「〜に答えて」**crucial role**「重要な役割」**world affairs**「国際問題」**up-and-coming entrepreneur**「成功が期待できる起業家」**international market**「国際市場」**in most situations**「大抵の場合」

 **Comprehension**

Read the essay and complete the sentences with the correct choices.

1. When people first meet and need to make small talk, it would be proper to _____.
   a. ask personal questions to get to know each other
   b. talk about recent events
   c. refrain from making comments on the topic
   d. avoid expressing your opinions and feelings

2. All of these statements have a similar meaning to "Don't take it personally" EXCEPT
_____.
   a. what I said doesn't apply to you personally
   b. I'm not insulting you
   c. it's not meant to be a personal attack on you
   d. I'm saying that your personal opinion makes me feel upset

3. In paragraph 2, the author mentions that _____.
   a. you can express your opinion or view on a relevant topic
   b. it's not a good idea to talk about a controversial topic
   c. you should offer your view on the topic even if you don't know enough about it
   d. if you don't have sufficient knowledge about the conversation topic, change the subject quickly

4. The author points out in the essay that _____.
   a. even if a person does not want to offer an opinion, he/she should respond to questions
   b. it's important to learn how to dodge a personal question while in conversation
   c. expressing yourself to others would help decrease cultural misunderstandings
   d. Western people prefer to discuss topics that cause arguments

Writing Practice

Rearrange the words and phrases in parentheses and make English sentences that correctly express the Japanese.

1. 新型スマホが、より安い価格のものを求める顧客の要求に応えて作られた。
   The new smartphone model was (response to / lower price / customer demand / for a / produced in).

   _____

   _____

2. 私たちは平和と繁栄の時代に生きていることを感謝しなければならない。
   We should be (in a time / and prosperity / be alive / of peace / grateful to).

   _____

   _____

3. タバコのポイ捨てを罰金制にすることは、環境汚染に対する社会的関心を引き起こす役割を担うかもしれない。
   Fining smokers (about environmental pollution / play a role / who litter might / public concern / in raising).

   _____

   _____

4. あまり答えたくないような立ち入った質問をされたら、「ごめん、プライベートなことなんで」と答えたらいいよ。
   When (you'd / not / nosy question / answer / asked a / rather), you can just say, "Sorry, that's a private matter."

   _____

   _____

Noteworthy Expressions

英語で自己表現できますか？

英語で自分の考えを表現するのはムリ！　と思っている人、いませんか？　でもこれからグローバル社会が広がっていくと、自分の考えや意見を表現することは避けては通れないかもしれませんね。苦手意識を克服して自分の考えや気持ちを上手に言い表すためのヒントをみてみましょう。これらは日本語で表現する場合でも参考になるかもしれません。日本文を参考にして、英語の下線部に、下の選択肢から適切な語句を選んで入れましょう。

1 　人前に出て話せるように、自分が思ったことを言葉にする練習をしておこう。
Practice putting what's on your mind into _____ so that you can be a good public speaker.

2 　日記を書くのは自己表現を身につけるのにいい方法である。
Keeping _____ is a good way to develop your ability to express yourself.

3 　自分を表現する場数をたくさん踏もう。
Get a lot of practical _____ expressing yourself.

4 　意見が食い違っていても、違った物の見方には耳を傾けよう。
Be open to different _____ even when you disagree with them.

5 　言葉だけで伝えようとするのではなく、顔の表現や身ぶり手ぶりも加えてみよう。
Don't restrict yourself to words but use facial expressions and _____.

6 　言いたいことを述べてから、そのあとで説明を補足していこう。
State the _____ of what you wish to say, and then fully explain it.

> views,　main idea,　a journal,　words,　gestures,　experience

▶◀ **Listening Practice**

Listen to the conversation and fill in the blanks with the appropriate words based on the conversation.

Kota recently started a homestay in the U.K., and the following conversation with his host mother occurs.

Mother: (   )?

   Kota: Pretty good. (   ) in my room.

Mother: That's wonderful. If there is anything you need, (   ).
Do you want to go to the store?

   Kota: No, (   ). What day of the week do you
usually do the family's laundry?

Mother: In our home, we all do our own laundry. You are welcome to (
). Do you know how to use it?

   Kota: Actually, I don't know. (   ).

▲▲ **Sharing Your Ideas**

1. What would you like your English teachers to do to help you improve your ability to express yourself? (Example: I would like my English teachers to use more group work.)

2. Suppose you are an up-and-coming entrepreneur. If you introduce a Japanese-style convenience store to the international market, how can you best sell the product? Talk with your partner and then present your ideas to the class. (Example: I will share the unique features of our convenience stores, e.g. they sell many kinds of ready-made meals and a wide variety of goods.)

UNIT 9 Prepare for Culture Shock

カルチャーショックに対処するには

Culture shock is a challenge that most global citizens face. Culture shock is the feelings of excitement, confusion, and frustration that accompany living in a foreign culture. It is caused by tasting different food, having new experiences, speaking a second language, and adjusting to a new set of cultural norms. When you experience culture shock, how do you deal with it?

Case Study

 59

First, look at the four-frame cartoon below, then discuss the question at the bottom of the cartoon with a partner or in small groups.

Chihiro and Luke are talking on campus in the U.S. Luke was in Japan for one year.

Question What suggestions would you propose to help Chihiro overcome homesickness?

 **Key Vocabulary**

Write the letter of the word or phrase with the closest meaning next to the appropriate vocabulary word.

1. guideline ( )   5. fluent ( )   9. phenomenon ( )
2. stage ( )   6. modify ( )   10. isolated ( )
3. entire ( )   7. appreciate ( )
4. unreliable ( )   8. reverse ( )

a. opposite	**b.** proficient	**c.** occurrence	**d.** instructions	**e.** separated
f. phase	**g.** undependable	**h.** change	**i.** understand	**j.** whole

 **Reading**

1 There are four stages of culture shock. While individuals experience these stages differently, they serve as general guidelines for how people learn to live in a new culture. The honeymoon stage is the time when a person is fascinated by the foreign culture. The person is excited by the food, customs, and exotic nature of the culture. For people who
5 make short trips, their entire journey can be like a honeymoon. The frustration stage involves feeling annoyed by the culture. People may become irritated and stressed by things such as unreliable public transportation and communication patterns.

2 The adjustment stage is when the person learns to adapt to the new culture. He/she becomes more fluent in the language and familiar with the customs. Finally, the
10 acceptance stage occurs when the person learns to accept the cultural differences and adapt to the culture. Since we learn cultural norms in a different manner from a young age, not everyone can reach this stage and broaden their own perspective.

3 Globalization has caused an increasing number of people to live in other countries for long periods of time. It takes a person a long time to adapt to a foreign culture, but
15 acceptance of different cultures also involves modifying one's own cultural perspective. For example, someone who lives in Japan for many years may eventually prefer Japanese cultural norms such as collectivism and harmony. He/She not only learns to appreciate the customs and traditions of another culture but also adjusts his/her own worldview. As a result, the person who returns to his/her home country may feel like an outsider and can
20 experience the phenomenon of reverse culture shock.

4 Culture shock is a natural process that most people experience while adapting to other cultures, so you don't have to view it negatively. When you feel lonely, isolated, or stressed, don't feel like you have no support. Your friends and college counselor are

available to help you. You can also use the phone or Internet to contact your family and
25 friends. Learn the language and customs by communicating with various people and
broadening your own perspective by acquiring new cultural norms. The experience of
culture shock is ultimately a good opportunity to expand your own horizons and will
help you become a global citizen.

■ NOTES

「カルチャーショック」の適応過程は学者によって多少の表現の違いがあるが、ここでは、**honeymoon
stage**（ハネムーン期）, **frustration stage**（フラストレーション期）, **adjustment stage**（適応移行期）,
acceptance stage（受容期）という表現を用いた。**serve as**「としての役割を果たす」**feel annoyed**「いら
立ちを感じる」**reverse culture shock**「逆カルチャーショック」**collectivism**「集団主義」**outsider**「よそ
者」**increasing number of**「ますます多くの」

Comprehension

Read the essay and complete the sentences with the correct choices.

1. While living in other countries for long periods of time, each person _____.
    a. becomes irritated and stressed by culture shock equally
    b. struggles in completely different ways to learn to live in a new culture
    c. is surely annoyed before being excited by the foreign culture
    d. experiences four stages of culture shock in different ways

2. When a person learns to accept the cultural differences and adapt to the culture, it
might be said that he/she _____.
    a. is in the final stage of culture shock
    b. needs to become more fluent in the language
    c. can reach four stages of culture shock
    d. rejects the culture

3. When you return to Japan after long-term study abroad, you might feel _____.
    a. four stages of culture shock
    b. Japanese cultural norms
    c. reverse culture shock
    d. collectivism and harmony

4. To deal with culture shock, the author mentions all of the following EXCEPT to _____.
    a. use the phone or Internet to contact your family and friends
    b. consider it positively
    c. fight against isolation
    d. talk with your friends and counselor

Rearrange the words and phrases in parentheses and make English sentences that correctly express the Japanese.

1. 私はその国に数年住んでいたときに、強烈なカルチャーショックに襲われた。

   I experienced (a couple of years / when I spent / culture shock / extreme) in the country.

   _____

   _____

2. 学生センターは、世界中からやってきた学生がコミュニケーションをとる場所として役立っている。

   The Student Center (from all over / a communication place / who are / serves as / for the students) the world.

   _____

   _____

3. 会議でのあなたの役割は他人の意見を聞くだけでなく、自分の信じることを発言することでもある。

   Your role at the conference is (to express / others' opinions / but also / to listen to / not only) what you believe.

   _____

   _____

4. このサービスは世界中だれでも無料で利用できる。

   This service is (for / the world / around / everyone / available to) free.

   _____

   _____

こんなところがカルチャーショック

良くも悪くも、異なる生活様式の中では誰もが受けるカルチャーショック。来日した外国人たちは、日本のどんなところにカルチャーショックを受けているでしょうか。一方で、海外に行った日本人の場合はどうでしょうか。その一例をみてみましょう。日本文を参考にして、英語の下線部に、下の選択肢から適切な語句を選んで入れましょう。

来日した外国人たちは、日本のこんなところにカルチャーショックを受ける

1　日本は伝統的な文化を大切にしている。
Japan cherishes _____ aspects of its culture.

2　女性専用車両がある。
There are _____ cars on trains.

3　自動販売機がどこにでもある。
You'll find _____ machines everywhere.

日本人は海外のこんなところにカルチャーショックを受ける

4　日本のことは、日本人が思っているほど知られていない。
People know _____ about Japan than Japanese think they do.

5　レストランで自分が食べ残した物を持って帰る。
They take _____ food home from a restaurant.

6　率直な物言いをする。思ったことをズバズバ言う。
People do not hesitate to express their opinions. They tell it like _____ .

> less,　vending,　traditional,　leftover,　it is,　women-only

Listening Practice

Listen to the conversation and fill in the blanks with the appropriate words based on the conversation.

Satomi is talking to Michael, who is an exchange student from Canada. Michael has been living in Kyoto for one year and will study in Japan for a few more years.

Satomi: Hey, Michael. I remember you were very homesick and

(   ).

Michael: I did feel (   )

due to cultural differences.

Satomi: What has helped (   )?

Michael: When I first came to Japan, (   )

that meets monthly. We still meet.

Satomi: That's great. What do you talk about?

Michael: We talk about the things we like about Japan and the things that frustrate us.

Together, we talk about ways (   ).

Satomi: It sounds like (   ).

Michael: It is. Thanks for asking.

Sharing Your Ideas

1. Suppose you're going to live overseas for a while. To decrease the amount of culture shock you could have while living in the country/place, what preparations could you make before you leave Japan? Present your idea to the class. (Example: I'm going to Maryland, USA. I'll prepare well so that I'm able to explain Japanese culture and history to people there in simple English.)

2. What information should Japan provide to people from overseas before they come to Japan so they can adjust to Japanese culture? Talk about it with your partner and present what you discussed in class. (Example: When you live in a community, you need to follow the rules of the community such as throwing away garbage in a specific trash area on a particular date and time. People who neglect the rules are seen as troublemakers.)

Overcome Communication Gaps in This Way

Global citizens can face communication barriers when they interact with others. As previously mentioned, there are language rules and customs that native speakers naturally follow, but they are not usually taught in textbooks and foreign language classrooms. This unit will discuss how communication barriers occur and how you can overcome those gaps.

Case Study

66

First, look at the four-frame cartoon below, then discuss the question at the bottom of the cartoon with a partner or in small groups.

During a break between classes, Mayumi is chatting with Steve, an exchange student from the U.S.

Question	Which opinion do you support, Mayumi's or Steve's?

 **Key Vocabulary**

 67

Write the letter of the word or phrase with the closest meaning next to the appropriate vocabulary word.

1. barrier   (   )   5. significant   (   )   9. perplexing   (   )

2. distinction   (   )   6. overcome   (   )   10. optimistic   (   )

3. context   (   )   7. encounter   (   )

4. explicitly   (   )   8. face-to-face   (   )

a. difference	**b.** considerable	**c.** positive	**d.** obstacle	**e.** in person
f. clearly	**g.** confusing	**h.** defeat	**i.** meet	**j.** background

Reading

 68~71

1 Cultural differences related to customs and values increase communication barriers. One example is the distinction between hierarchical and egalitarian cultures. A person from a hierarchical culture will naturally feel more comfortable addressing acquaintances by their last name and title rather than first names. High- and low-context cultures are
5   another example which relates to the discussion of non-verbal communication. A "high-context culture" is a culture where everyone shares a common background and cultural norms. In contrast, in a "low-context culture" people do not share the same background and perspective, so it is common to express things explicitly.

2 Non-verbal behavior also can cause communication barriers to develop. Language
10   learners are instructed about the grammar, vocabulary, and pronunciation of the second language. However, they are not always given the chance to learn about and practice non-verbal communication. It is a fact that a significant percentage of communication is non-verbal. People express themselves through facial expressions, eye contact, tone of voice, gestures, and personal space. Therefore, it is essential to pay attention to non-
15   verbal cues as you converse with people. Noticing how people use gestures and attempting to mimic their behavior and tone would make communication smoother.

3 There are clues as to how you can overcome communication barriers. When you do not share a common language and culture with others, try to learn the language rules and customs of others. If you encounter unknown words or expressions in face-to-face or
20   computer-mediated communication, start investigating things that you find perplexing. Use your phone to take notes on these things, and if a native speaker is near you, ask him/her to explain the meaning. People naturally have different personalities, so try to accept their beliefs and values as you communicate. Learn to appreciate different cultural norms such as interpreting facial expressions and ways of making eye contact. The

25 Internet, television, and film are other good sources of data to help you reduce communication barriers.

4 You should not think pessimistically about communication barriers. Be optimistic and learn to seek out opportunities to actively communicate with others. Don't be discouraged even if you face various communication barriers. The experience of
30 encountering cultural barriers will surely give you a chance to develop as an adept communicator.

■ NOTES

hierarchical「階層的な、上下関係のある」**egalitarian**「平等主義の」**title**「肩書」**high- and low-context cultures**「ハイ・ローコンテクスト文化：（ハイコンテクスト文化は文脈、背景、言外の意味を、ローコンテクスト文化は言葉そのものの意味を重視する）」**non-verbal communication**「言葉を使わないコミュニケーション」**a significant percentage of**「かなりの割合の」**personal space**「個人空間（他人に侵入されると不快に感じる自分の周囲の心理的な縄張り空間）」**mimic**「まねる」**face-to-face or computer-mediated communication**「対面形式あるいはコンピューターを利用したコミュニケーション」**sources of data**「情報源」**seek out**「探し求める」**adept communicator**「コミュニケーションがとても上手な人」

𝒞 Comprehension

Read the essay and complete the sentences with the correct choices.

1. It can be inferred that hierarchical cultures _____.
   a. value relationships between superiors and inferiors
   b. have been extremely successful in the U.S.
   c. consider the idea that all people are equal most important
   d. intend to share a common background and cultural norms

2. A high-context culture uses language _____.
   a. that shows thoughts or feelings clearly
   b. to emphasize the use of eye contact while speaking
   c. to express beliefs and values as directly as possible
   d. in a way that heavily relies on the context of the conversation

3. The author of the essay recommends using a _____ to take notes on unknown words or expressions.
   a. dictionary   **b.** notebook
   c. personal computer   **d.** smartphone

4. The essay advises you to be _____ if you confront communication barriers.
   a. doubtful   **b.** sympathetic
   c. positive   **d.** indifferent

Rearrange the words and phrases in parentheses and make English sentences that correctly express the Japanese.

1. 個人空間に配慮するために、近寄り過ぎるのは避けてください。
   You should (to respect / getting / personal space / too close / avoid).

   _____

   _____

2. 人の口調は時によって言葉で表現されることよりももっと多くのことを表すことがある。
   The tone of voice (express more / is expressed verbally / than what / can sometimes).

   _____

   _____

3. ローコンテクスト文化では、ほとんどのメッセージは言葉を手がかりにして伝えられる。
   Most (in a low-context / in verbal cues / are conveyed / messages) culture.

   _____

   _____

4. 日本に関するレポートを書くために、トムは上下関係の文化に関する情報をインターネットでたくさん集めた。
   To write a paper about Japan, Tom gathered (concerning / through / hierarchical cultures / a lot of information) the Internet.

   _____

   _____

Noteworthy Expressions

あるあるコミュニケーションギャップ

アメリカ人 A さんが日本に来て思ったことを取り上げてみました。以下の J さんの発言は、それに対する日本人の考えの一例です。相手が異なった理解の仕方をしていたり、十分な情報をもたないで判断していた場合は、そのままにしておくと誤解されたまま双方の間でコミュニケーションギャップを作っていくことになるかもしれません。そこで、自分なりの考えを相手に伝えて、相互理解を深めていけるような会話例を 3 つ取り上げてみました。次の日本文をみて、合致した内容の英文になるように、英語の下線部に、下の選択肢から適切な語句を選んで入れましょう。

1. A: 日本人は親切だけど、フレンドリーではない。
   J: 基本的には日本人はフレンドリーなんだけど、自己表現力が足りないかも。

   A: Japanese are _____ but not friendly.

   J: Japanese are basically friendly, but many people may _____ the ability to express themselves.

2. A: 日本人は白熱した議論を好まない。
   J: 我々はただ、不必要な衝突を避けているだけだ。自分の意見を主張するより意見の一致を求める。

   A: Japanese don't like having very _____ discussions.

   J: We just avoid unnecessary conflict. We often seek _____ rather than assert our own opinions.

3. A: 人の目を気にし過ぎる傾向があるのが理解できない。
   J: もしも他人がどう思うか気にしないと、配慮に欠けるやつだと思われる。

   A: I don't understand the Japanese tendency to _____ what others think.

   J: If you don't care about what other people think, people will think you are too _____.

   ---
   consensus, inconsiderate, lack, heated, kind, worry about

Listen to the conversation and fill in the blanks with the appropriate words based on the conversation.

Mark is an exchange student who is studying in Japan. He is speaking with Shiho after class. He asks her why many Japanese college students live with their family and commute from their house.

Mark: When teenagers enter college in the U.S., they live independently.

Shiho: (   )?

Mark: What I'm saying is that students in the U.S. usually leave home and live in a dorm or (   ).

Shiho: Are you saying that Japanese students don't leave home because (   )?

Mark: That's right.

Shiho: I think you've misunderstood Japanese students and Japanese society. (   ) with dorms, and it's easy for them to commute using public transportation. Also, it's customary to (   ).

Mark: Oh, is that right? I thought they were afraid to (   ).

Sharing Your Ideas

1. Propose some ways to improve communication with people from other backgrounds. (Example: When I'm not sure what the other person says, I'll ask, "Let me clarify my understanding." When we don't know enough of each other's language, I'll try to use gestures to communicate.)

2. Brainstorm some creative ideas with your partner about how to break down the communication gaps in the following situation.
   While you are working part time as a restaurant server or a convenience-store clerk, what kinds of communication gaps might occur between you and another employee who has a different culture from yours? How could you decrease those gaps? Present the ideas you discussed with a partner to the class. (Example: Using English with another non-native employee could cause communication problems. When this happens, we can use a smartphone translation app to help us have a smooth conversation.

UNIT 11 Effective Ways to Reduce Stress

ストレスを減らす方法とは

People who live abroad often feel stress due to the new environment, customs, lifestyle differences, and so on. It is natural to feel irritated about different aspects of life abroad such as unfamiliar food, inconveniences in daily life, and easygoing attitudes. Therefore, you may well suffer from some kinds of stress while you study abroad. But you can surely learn ways to relieve stress and adapt to life there. Have confidence that you can certainly get through tough times and try to remain calm and not stressed.

▼ Case Study

 73

First, look at the four-frame cartoon below, then discuss the question at the bottom of the cartoon with a partner or in small groups.

Mike is an exchange student from Australia. He is talking with his friend, Wakana, about stressful aspects of life in Japan.

Question What do you think would help Mike release stress?

_____

_____

 **Key Vocabulary** 74

Write the letter of the word or phrase with the closest meaning next to the appropriate vocabulary word.

1. participation ( )   5. establish ( )   9. multiple ( )
2. crack ( )   6. routine ( )   10. access ( )
3. pressure ( )   7. sufficient ( )
4. accomplish ( )   8. embrace ( )

a. achieve	**b.** adopt	**c.** joining	**d.** acquire	**e.** daily schedule
f. split	**g.** wide variety of	**h.** create	**i.** enough	**j.** strain

 Reading 75~78

1 The most stressful part of living abroad is that life is unfamiliar. When studying abroad, the style of participation in classes and communication are very different from Japan. Students are required to study harder. You might be expected to act in the same way as the local students at the university or institution where you entered. Possibly, you
5 could almost crack due to the pressure caused by these high expectations. But keep remembering the key factors that influenced your decision to study abroad, and keep making an effort to accomplish your goal. Therefore, it is wise to establish a routine to your life while challenging yourself with new experiences.

2 At the same time, you may wish to make a bucket list of things you want to do while
10 you are in the country. When you feel homesick and need a refreshing change, try eating Japanese foods, doing a new sport or activity, and taking a leisurely walk. Make time for hobbies, interests, and relaxation. Getting enough sleep might help you relax and release stress as well. The time in the country is limited and you should try to take advantage of various opportunities.

15 **3** There are some other things to keep in mind to reduce stress. Rather than constantly compare life in Japan and life abroad, learn to embrace the new culture and enjoy your time there. In the meantime, you may gain a greater appreciation for parts of life in Japan you took for granted. When you feel annoyed with something in a new culture, talk about your frustration with a friend so you can better understand the situation.

20 **4** Remember the various ways you will grow as a person through the experience of tackling stress. Spend time with friends and share your worries with them. The Internet provides us with multiple ways to access information about other cultures and interact with people, but online communication can never replicate the experience of living

abroad. You will mature and learn to alter your own worldview with the experiences
25 gained from life in the local area. The process of adjusting to life abroad and learning to
manage stress will also help you in the future when you are applying for jobs.

■ NOTES
establish a routine「いつも決まって行うことを定着させる」 bucket list「達成したいことを書き出したリ
スト」 refreshing change「気分転換」 make time for「〜する時間を持つ」 take advantage of「をうまく
活用する」 take for granted「当たり前だと思う」 tackle stress「ストレスに対処する」 replicate「再現する」

Comprehension

Read the essay and complete the sentences with the correct choices.

1. While studying abroad, you might _____ because you can't meet expectations.
   a. buckle under the pressure
   b. participate in classes actively
   c. make an effort to reach your goal
   d. feel bored by the daily routine

2. The author recommends you to _____ when you need a refreshing change.
   a. wake up earlier in the morning
   b. try a new activity
   c. realize your own strength
   d. attempt the impossible

3. Living abroad may give you a chance to rediscover the good parts of life in Japan that
   you _____.
   a. considered valuable
   b. highly praised all the time
   c. took particular notice of
   d. regarded as quite natural

4. Through the experiences you gain from life overseas, you will _____.
   a. get more time to spend with local friends
   b. find multiple ways to access information on the Internet
   c. learn to interact with people online
   d. change your perspective of the world

Rearrange the words and phrases in parentheses and make English sentences that correctly express the Japanese.

1. 私は気分転換が必要なときは、愛犬と散策する。
   I (beloved dog / a refreshing change / I need / when / with my / take a walk).

   _____

   _____

2. 朝いつも決まってすることを定着させると、一日の時間をうまく使うのに役立つ。
   Establishing a (wisely throughout / would help / your time / morning routine / you use) the day.

   _____

   _____

3. 私は新しい言語を学ぶのに、インターネットをうまく活用したい。
   I want to (a new language / of online opportunities / to learn / take advantage).

   _____

   _____

4. 停電になったときに、私はどれだけ電気を当たり前のものと考えていたか分かった。
   I realized (for granted / a power outage / I took electricity / when I had / how much).

   _____

   _____

Noteworthy Expressions

こんなことがストレスに

海外から日本にやってきた留学生はどんなことにストレスを感じるでしょうか。また、海外に出かけた日本人留学生の場合はどうでしょうか。いくつかの例をみてストレスを軽くすることを考えてみましょう。次の日本文をみて、I feel stress に続けた英文が日本語の内容に合致するように、英語の下線部に、下の選択肢から適切な語句を選んで入れましょう。1～3は海外からの留学生が日本でストレスを感じる場合、4～6は日本人の留学生が海外でストレスを感じる場合の例文です。

私は ＿＿＿＿＿ にストレスを感じる。　I feel stress ＿＿＿＿＿.

1 駅やレストランの自動券売機の使い方にまごついたとき
when I am ＿＿＿＿＿ about how to use an automatic ticket machine at railway stations and restaurants

2 案内表示が日本語だけで書かれていて意味が分からないとき
when ＿＿＿＿＿ are written only in Japanese and I can't understand the meaning

3 相手が自分の思っていることをはっきりと言わないので何を考えているか分からないとき
when I have ＿＿＿＿＿ what the person is thinking since the person doesn't express his/her thoughts clearly

4 現地の言葉でうまく気持ちを伝えることができないとき
when I can't ＿＿＿＿＿ my thoughts to people in the local language

5 授業中、自分の意見を言うことを求められるとき
when I am ＿＿＿＿＿ to express my opinion in class

6 自己主張の強い人と接しないといけないとき
when I need to deal with very ＿＿＿＿＿ people

signs,　convey,　opinionated,　confused,　required,　no idea

▶◀ **Listening Practice**

Listen to the conversation and fill in the blanks with the appropriate words based on the conversation.

Tiffany and Kenji take the same class at a university in the U.S. They are having lunch after class when the following conversation occurs.

Tiffany: Many students feel stressed out at this midpoint in the semester. How about you?

Kenji: I do. (   ) and a paper due the following week. In order to relax, (   ) when I was in Japan.

Tiffany: That sounds nice. Taking a drive somewhere close to school is also (   ).

Kenji: Unfortunately, I have no car.

Tiffany: Even if you don't have a car, (   ) to relieve stress on campus.

Kenji: What do you suggest?

Tiffany: (   ) every week. Would you like to join me next time?

Kenji: Sounds great! (   )?

▲ **Sharing Your Ideas**

1. How do you relieve stress from dealing with people and studying? Present one of your ways to reduce stress to the class. (Example: Listening to songs by my favorite artist is a great way to release stress.)

2. People from overseas sometimes feel that Japanese are very busy and need to create spare time to live a more laid-back or stress-free lifestyle. What do you think of this view? Talk with your partner about whether you agree or disagree and present your ideas to the class. (Example: -I agree. The Japanese government is promoting work-life balance initiatives, but not many employees have got benefits from the reforms yet and have been forced to work overtime. I think they need more time to chill out. -I disagree. I think they enjoy having free time thanks to a five-day work week.)

UNIT 12 Have a Positive Way of Thinking

グローバル社会を前向き思考で

Positive thinking is the attitude that a situation will have favorable results and not getting discouraged when plans do not proceed as expected. It means repeatedly trying and refusing to accept defeat. Someone with an optimistic attitude focuses more on the good and positive in a situation and less on the negative. Those with this frame of mind neither accept defeat nor allow negativity to affect their mood. This unit encourages you to become a positive thinker.

▼ Case Study

80

First, look at the four-frame cartoon below, then discuss the question at the bottom of the cartoon with a partner or in small groups.

Kaoru is an exchange student from Japan. She is talking with her friend, David, after class.

Question What do you think Kaoru should do to be more optimistic?

Write the letter of the word or phrase with the closest meaning next to the appropriate vocabulary word.

1. outcome   (   )   5. quote   (   )   9. demanding   (   )
2. capture   (   )   6. anticipated   (   )   10. regret   (   )
3. beneficial (   )   7. pessimistic   (   )
4. upbeat   (   )   8. mature   (   )

| a. negative | b. difficult | c. feel sorry | d. grow | e. catch |
| f. citation | g. result | h. expected | i. favorable | j. cheerful |

 Reading 82~85

1 This textbook has discussed many of the challenging and exciting aspects of living in a global world. The best advice to keep in mind while abroad is to be a positive thinker wherever and however you live. A positive thinker is a person who is optimistic about the outcome of various situations. The expression "glass half full" captures an optimist's

5 way of seeing things. When the optimistic person sees half a glass of water, he/she views it as "half full" rather than "half empty."

2 Optimistic thinking is beneficial because it helps the person remain upbeat rather than depressed. The British Christian writer C.S. Lewis once said, "failures are finger posts on the road to achievement." Keeping this quote in mind, you should be optimistic even

10 when the outcome is different from the one you hoped for or anticipated. One piece of advice to remember when you are facing many challenging situations is to talk with various people. They would surely offer you a variety of perspectives from different standpoints which might become your finger posts.

3 Living abroad can cause a person to become depressed and pessimistic. For example,

15 you may not be able to express yourself completely at a party or dinner with your host family. Try not to criticize yourself for remaining silent during the dinner because you could not express everything you wanted to say. Instead of keeping this negative frame of mind, remember that the experience of talking with others is improving your ability to communicate. While listening to their conversation, you are also learning about another

20 perspective and maturing into a global citizen. Therefore, you don't have to feel depressed and dwell on the negative even if you can't join in the conversation. A positive thinker will feel blessed for the opportunity to face this demanding social situation.

4 On the other hand, you would definitely regret the decision in the future if you avoid social situations because you are worried too much about the outcome. Adopting an optimistic attitude will unquestionably help you thrive in a global world. You should take the initiative to solve complex problems and continue to take on new challenges. Living a life of ups and downs is sometimes tough, but one needs to have some positive thinking all the time. This perspective will help you become a global person who will positively contribute to our international society.

■ NOTES

positive thinker「前向きな思考の人間」**C.S. Lewis**「(1898-1963) イギリスの作家、神学者。著書の『ナルニア国ものがたり』(**The Chronicles of Narnia**) は特に有名」**finger post**「道しるべ」**frame of mind**「気持ちの持ちよう」**dwell on the negative**「否定的なことをくよくよと考える」**take the initiative**「率先してやる」**continue to take on new challenges**「新しいことに挑戦し続ける」**life of ups and downs**「山あり谷ありの人生」

🎗 Comprehension

Read the essay and complete the sentences with the correct choices.

1. According to the essay, if you see a glass as half full, you would tend to _____.
   a. think positively
   b. have a pessimistic view of life
   c. take things logically
   d. focus on the bad things at all times

2. The essay tells you that failures _____.
   a. are a different part of success
   b. serve as a guide to accomplishing something
   c. show the direction to a certain place
   d. are crucial for your life

3. The author points out that you _____ even if you can't join in the conversation at a party.
   a. should spend a lot of time listening to others
   b. should make an effort to express yourself
   c. don't have to be discouraged
   d. don't have to behave modestly

4. To thrive in a global world, you need all the following EXCEPT _____.
   a. to adopt an optimistic attitude
   b. to take the initiative to solve complex problems
   c. having a positive way of thinking
   d. worrying too much about how things turn out

Writing Practice

Rearrange the words and phrases in parentheses and make English sentences that correctly express the Japanese.

1. さまざまな国からの学生が現在、私たちの機関で日本語を勉強している。
   Students (are currently / in our / countries / from / studying Japanese / a variety of) institute.

---

2. 彼女のアドバイスのおかげで、私は勉強に集中することができた。
   I was able to (thanks to / concentrate on / advice from / a piece of / my studies) her.

---

3. 議論のあとの気まずい沈黙を避けるために、私は率先してみんなに新しい話題を提供した。
   I took (a new topic / and brought up / an awkward silence / the initiative / to avoid) after the argument.

---

4. 彼は IT（情報技術）を活用して、いつも熱心に新しいことに挑戦している。
   He is (new challenges / to take on / information technology / always eager / utilizing).

Noteworthy Expressions

きみの人生、前向きで！

くじけそうなときや困難なことに直面することは多々あります。これからグローバルに生きていくときには更に壁にぶち当たるかもしれません。そんなときに自分を励まし、ネガティブな思いに打ち勝っていくヒントを集めてみました。日本文を参考にして、英語の下線部に、下の選択肢から適切な語句を選んで入れましょう。

1 過去の過ちを何度も頭の中で思い返すのはやめよう。
Stop _____ past mistakes in your head.

2 日常生活には困難なことや問題があるのは当たり前のことだと受け止めよう。
Accept _____ that there are difficulties and problems in everyday life.

3 自分の気持ちを親しい人に話してみよう。
Talk over your thoughts with someone _____ you.

4 瞑想したり祈ったりして、あなたのまわりのものや人に感謝しよう。
Meditate or pray and be _____ the things and people around you.

5 絶対大丈夫、と自分に言い聞かせよう。
Tell yourself that you'll be fine _____.

6 遊びや趣味の時間をスケジュールに入れておこう。
Schedule time for _____ activities.

7 今日はついていると思おう。
Think today is _____.

> my day, replaying, leisure, thankful for, the fact, close to, for sure

Listen to the conversation and fill in the blanks with the appropriate words based on the conversation.

Shigeru and Megan are colleagues at a global company in Tokyo. They are conversing about working in a global world.

Shigeru: So (   )?

Megan: It was hard at first, but now I'm very happy here.

Shigeru: (   )?

Megan: I found it hard to make friends, but (   ).

Shigeru: That's good. I'm glad that you didn't take it personally when (   ).

Megan: (   ) who doesn't get depressed easily.

Shigeru: (   )!

1. Are you more of an optimistic or pessimistic person? Why do you think so? (Example: I think I'm a pessimistic person because I worry that a situation might have a bad outcome in many cases.)

2. In order to become a more optimistic person, what are some things you'll do in your daily life to reach this goal? Consider the information you've learned in this unit as you create an answer. Talk with your partner and present a couple of things you would do to the class. (Example: I won't be too hard on myself when I have trouble communicating in English.)

テキストの Key Vocabulary を語尾から語頭へと -c, -ed, -rd のように、アルファベティカルに逆配列した語彙集です。同じ語尾で終わる語彙をまとめていますので、単語を区別して覚えるのに役立てましょう。数字はその単語が出てくる Unit を示します。

pessimistic	12	atmosphere	6	establish	11	conduct	3
optimistic	10	entire	9	accomplish	11	product	1
isolated	9	pressure	11	break	7	regret	12
anticipated	12	mature	12	crack	11	interpret	4
regard	3	capture	12	beneficial	12	outfit	5
awkward	8	gesture	6	controversial	8	insult	4
face-to-face	10	increase	3	essential	2	significant	10
embrace	11	likewise	3	individual	4	immigrant	6
notice	7	reverse	9	criticism	4	resident	1
appearance	5	converse	7	broaden	3	sufficient	11
acquaintance	5	appreciate	9	maintain	6	compliment	5
confidence	1	appropriate	8	impression	1	current	8
preference	6	cooperate	2	possession	5	fluent	9
conference	3	hesitate	4	participation	11	assert	2
influence	4	quote	12	expectation	6	latest	5
resource	2	contribute	2	connection	1	adjust	4
reduce	8	unique	8	distinction	10	context	10
employee	3	achieve	7	solution	2	complex	8
beverage	4	thrive	1	phenomenon	9	modify	9
encourage	7	expensive	1	similar	6	strategy	8
stage	9	effective	5	career	3	gradually	7
unreliable	9	perspective	2	barrier	10	reply	5
enable	1	attentive	7	encounter	10	explicitly	10
desirable	2	resolve	6	deliver	6	consequently	7
struggle	8	observe	7	occur	3	military	8
multiple	11	criticize	3	access	11	personality	5
overcome	10	analyze	2	jealous	5	opportunity	2
outcome	12	demanding	12	upbeat	12	popularity	1
guideline	9	stimulating	7	impact	1	diversity	6
routine	11	perplexing	10	conflict	4	honesty	4

TEXT PRODUCTION STAFF

edited by	編集
Mitsugu Shishido	宍戸　貢

cover design by	表紙デザイン
Nobuyoshi Fujino	藤野　伸芳

text design by	本文デザイン
ALIUS	アリウス

illustrated by	イラスト
Kyosuke Kuromaru	黒丸　恭介

CD PRODUCTION STAFF

narrated by	吹き込み者
Karen Haedrich (Ame E)	カレン・ヘドリック (アメリカ英語)
Chris Koprowski (Ame E)	クリス・コプロスキ (アメリカ英語)

Surviving in a Global World
グローバル社会をどう生きるか

2020年1月10日　初版印刷
2022年3月25日　第3刷発行

著　　者　　中川　準治　Justin Charlebois

発 行 者　　佐野　英一郎

発 行 所　　株式会社 成美堂
　　　　　　〒101-0052　東京都千代田区神田小川町3-22
　　　　　　TEL 03-3291-2261　FAX 03-3293-5490
　　　　　　https://www.seibido.co.jp

印 刷・製 本　　倉敷印刷株式会社

ISBN 978-4-7919-7209-8　　　　　　　　　　　　Printed in Japan